MADE DIFFERENT

FINDING PURPOSE FOR WOMEN.

"There is nothing more rare, nor more beautiful,
than a woman being unapologetically herself:
comfortable in her perfect imperfection…
That is the true essence of beauty."
Steve Maraboli

WINIFRED AYANDA

Copyright © 2017 by Winifred Ayanda

Published in Lagos, Nigeria by **Horlartech publishers.**
Surulere Lagos Nigeria.
Email:horlartechng@yahoo.com
Telephone: +234 - 806 - 4468 - 167

Art direction and cover design: **Horlartech impressions.**
Inside layout: **Sebicon Concept**
Production: **Horlartech impressions..**

FOREWORD

I am so elated that at last this beloved sister of mine has invested her precious time in weaving together her life transforming thoughts into a book that will change the life of many generations that will be privileged to read it.

My husband has told me several times of your visionary leadership of the Breakingforth International Christian Center [BICC] women ministry and how your commitment helped the ministry chart through troubled waters. So it didn't come to me as a surprise that you are writing about women which I believe are the experience you have gathered from your years of leading women.

You have been tested by fire, stood, learnt a lot from your tests, grew through them and still you continue to grow. Of course we know that to make a difference you must be that difference that you intend to make in the lives of others. God intention for creating the woman is not to be superior or inferior to a man; but to be a help meet to Him if when that man finds His woman. To be a help meet is a higher calling! It means to be a whole woman spirit, soul and body. It means also that woman is empowered and equipped to help her man become all that God has called him to be and at the same time nurture a whole generation. Unfortunately in the past and even in the present age people still view the woman as inferior to the man when it was never God's intention to make any of the sexes lesser than the other.

Winifred has help to shed some light on the woman and purpose and how without it she will never be able to discover her identity and fulfill her assignment on the earth. The author highlighted in detail Genesis 1:27 in this book of how men and women were created in the image of God which in Hebrew is "Imago Dei." The author likewise made us to understand that most women were unable to make a difference because of the unpleasant circumstances they found themselves either by birth, geographical location or by marriage.

It takes sacrifice and focus to maintain what you are designed by God to be. It requires you to move with the right people, hear the right word and be at the right place. Determine in your heart to make a difference like great women such as Margaret Thatcher, Mother Theresa, Indra Ghandi, and their likes.

I have read this book and sincerely recommend it to women of all ages, creed and race anywhere. Buy a copy, read and study until you get the light in it.

Thank you Winifred for this book we are proud of you because you are already making a difference!

Evang. Stephanie Cherry Olubowale
Savannah, GA
USA

DEDICATION.

This book is dedicated to every woman who desires to break stereotypes, dares to pursue her purpose and change her world.

ACKNOWLEDGMENTS

GOD, the one who has made my pen, the pen of a ready writer; every step of the way; your gentle spirit led me through until the very last word. I thank you Lord.

To my love, my life, my heartbeat; baby you have been there for me through the highs and lows, your unflinching love and belief in my abilities is my inspiration.

To the my lovely kids, every day I look at you three, you give me reasons to go on and make sure I live my purpose so you all can live yours.

To my amazing sister, Dr Titi and her husband Dr Churchill (my dear brother) who brought my dream to life, I say a very big thank you, because of you both, millions have the opportunity to be inspired and dare to pursue purpose.

To my twin sister, Dr. Faith, your tireless effort in the proof reading of this material is highly appreciated.

To my presiding pastor at my local assembly, BICC, Pastor David and his charming and graceful wife; First Lady Stephanie, a true woman of purpose, you believed in me, prayed for and with me, and to you both I say thank you.

To everyone who helped me one way or the other in the process of getting this book out, you are deeply appreciated.

CONTENTS.

Chapter

1

I AM THE SUM TOTAL OF WHO I AM, WHOSE I AM AND WHO I AM CALLED TO BE.

WHO AM I

'So God created man in His own image, in the image of God created he him, male and female created He them."
GEN 1:27

Who am I ?

I t can be tough growing up as a girl, its as though there seems to be some secret mission to ensure you don't fulfill purpose. From the moment you are born you are given restrictions, limitations, boundaries. People already have pre construed ideas as to who you should and should not be, what you should and should not do. Growing up as a girl you are told how to behave, what society expects of you, what your family demands from you. The liberty for self discovery and actualization is never yours to discern. Your definitions and identifications are almost never at your instance and seldom in your favour.

Consequently, many end up being defined by circumstances, societal demands, family expectations, friends etc. The truth is that we can never live fulfilled lives until we can first truly define who we are on our terms and this forms the bedrock for self actualization and fulfillment.

In most of my conferences and seminars where I teach on self discovery and purpose, I like to begin with this very salient but often under looked question.

"WHO ARE YOU?" and more often than not people hardly have a clue who they are. A few however respond by telling me their names.

Who am I ?

A name hardly passes as a definition of who you are; people change their names as quickly as people change shoes and bags, married women do that on a regular basis. I've met with people who tell me that they had to change their names because they didn't feel it represented their personality or they simply didn't like the sound or the meaning of the name.

Now, don't get me wrong a name can in fact be an integral pointer and reference to self actualization but it is not the focal nor determiner of purpose. You make your name and not the other way around. Once purpose is discovered, a name can be christened as a form of acknowledgment of the fulfillment of that actualization. We have seen several examples in biblical times. In the case of Abraham when he was to be the father of many nations, his name was changed from Abram to Abraham. The same for Sarah, from Sarai to Sarah, Jacob to Israel, Saul to Paul, the list is endless. Your name responds to your purpose and not your purpose responding to your name. Hence, your name doesn't define you at least not if it isn't tied to a definite consciousness of self discovery and purpose.

Until the notion of who you are is clearly understood especially as it pertains to a woman you would not be able to take your place in the grand scheme of things.

Who am I ?

So woman let's look critically at who you are and no better place to discover it than from the very beginning. At creation we are told that God formed the human species from the dust of the ground and breathed into its nostrils giving it the right of life. At this point humanity had only one expression in the form of masculinity and that lone expression wasn't adequate to undertake successfully all the functions, roles and responsibilities for the human species. In other words, the man by himself was inadequate invariably giving rise to the need to create another human expression that would complement the earlier human creation. In a nutshell, she was to make up for the shortfall.

The creation of this addition was going to be seamless, precise and painless and its fundamental prerequisite for authenticity and universal acceptance is that it must originate from the first human. In fact the first human would have to undergo a surgery for this purpose, asleep and oblivious of his surroundings.

The precise details of the surgery are contained in the book of Genesis. As that human slept a piece of his ribs was removed from him and constructed to form this much needed codicil. Equally interesting is the body part

Who am I ?

which was chosen in the creation of this human, who was called **WOMAN -:** "The ribs"

Some have argued ferociously that the ribs were chosen specifically by God for its location in the body ie the sides of the human frame to show that woman was to be side by the side of man and being equal. While that might be debatable we cannot overlook the scientific symbolism of the particular body part

> *Though we (Male and female) are uniquely different, essentially we are both the same. We both desire the same things… our strengths and weaknesses are different but no less superior or inferior, it's just different.*

based on the functions and characteristic of the ribs. Scientists have described the ribcage as what provides a strong framework onto which the muscles of the shoulders, girdle, chest, upper abdomen and back can attach. It is flexible. It can expand and contract by the actions of the muscles of respiration. Simply put, you cannot exist without your ribcage because of its enormous importance to the total existence and functionality of the human system. Now that might be a little bit extreme given the fact that the first man could exist without the woman hitherto , but whether he could function effectively without her is a completely different matter. We must not be oblivious of the strident fact that

Who am I ?

man by himself was at abyssal or meager performance until when he had the much needed assistance that came in the form of a woman. Even God concluded that it was all good!

The ribs give SUPPORT, FUNCTIONALITY, PROTECTION AND ASSISTANCE to the body.

Strong framework→→Attachment→→Flexibility.

The strong framework of the ribcage allows many organs to attach to the ribcage and function effectively. This is why women are usually gifted in multitasking; a woman can do a thousand and one things all at once because she has been structured that way from the beginning. Many things and people naturally attract and demand her attention and like wonder woman she's up for the challenge. Woman's
flexibility allows her to be wife, mother, business woman, career woman, home maker, community leader, nation builder and hold it all together. She can be anything for everyone at anytime.

She was to form the required support system that would make His creation complete. After woman was made, the creative process officially ended and because of her the human race would never cease, humanity's rite of

Who am I ?

passage would only come through a woman. People have argued and cited several instances for a long time that it's a man world when in fact it's a woman's world.

The earth that God created is personified as a woman; it is feminine because of its life giving and nurturing similarities. The human race would neither exist nor function effectively without a woman.

God created the human race in His image and he made them male and female, they are both different expressions of the same God. So even though male and female are uniquely different, essentially we are both the same. We mostly desire the same thing ie a good and fulfilling life.

In this light we should never see ourselves as competitors but collaborators with men. The competitive spirit is a negative one that tries to negate the beauty and original intent of God. We were to work as a team. Our (men and women) strengths and weaknesses are different but no less inferior or superior, it's just different.

I hate to describe women as weaker vessels I'd rather like to describe women as a different kind of vessel that is because women are usually termed weaker largely in

Who am I ?

7

terms of physical prowess and not intellectual or spiritual proficiency and it is in these areas that God connects with individuals. So we are different but certainly not weaker.

What most people fail to realize is that on the day that God created physical man, he had already created woman because woman already existed in man.

"In the day that God created man, in the likeness of God created he him, male and female created he them, and blessed them, AND CALLED THEIR NAME ADAM, in the day when they were created."

Genesis 5:2

Woman only became expressed differently out of man for functional purposes hence the different expression. God neither sees us as male or female but sees us as in our spiritual dimension- sexless-. God is both female and male. Woman understand this carefully, the sexist theory originated from cultural and societal traditions , it is neither based on spiritual nor Godly ethos and should not be construed or misrepresented as such

.

Women have infact been given very important roles and assignment even in biblical times, women have been made

rulers and judges in Israel long before it became a

<u>*Who am I ?*</u>

matter of political correctness , they had been ordained prophetess and given offices of spiritual prominence long before it became a topic of debate. The messiah was to be brought into this world through the exclusive rite of a woman without the typical assistance of her male counterpart, a first and certainly a last. During the messiah's earthly ministry, a group of women, Mary Magdalene, Joanna, Susanna and many others ministered to his needs and that of his ministry. When he eventually died and resurrected, it was a woman who became the first evangelist proclaiming his resurrection. The messiah, Jesus, placed a very high premium on woman then and still does.

It's easy to get caught up in these worldly expectations of you as a woman that you forget your individualistic purpose or assignment by God. Every woman struggles with that.

It was Betty Friedan who stated it eloquently and I quote.

"Each suburban wife struggles with it alone. As she made the beds, shopped for groceries, matched slipcovers materials ,ate peanut butter sandwiches with her children, chauffeured club scouts and brownies ,lay beside her husband at night- she was afraid to ask even herself the silent question-Is this all?"

Who am I ?

It's definitely not all. There's much more to you than what you have been taught or made to believe. That's why you must understand who you really are through the eyes of God
and see how a larger than life God can step out of eternity into time to pause and create you. You are definitely bigger than you think you are. Even the angels of God envy you, the principalities and powers question the authority and extreme privilege that have been given to you. They know that even though God has given them supernatural powers, humans were exclusively given glory and honour, you can read the full account in Psalms 8:4-8. Even they know that it's not about being female or male it's about understanding your role and position as a human being. The psalmist gave a very resounding and breath taking account of the thought process and tender loving intentions, zeal and care God has for you.

"Thou knowest my downsitting and mine uprising. Thou understandest my thought afar off. Thou compassest my path and my lying down and art acquitted with all my ways. For there is not a word in my tongue but,lo,O Lord thou knowest it all together.thou hast beset me before and behind and laid thy hands upon me. Such knowledge is too wonderful for me.it is high I cannot attain it." Psalms 139

Who am I ?

Our physical presence on earth actually sprung from a spiritual experience in heaven. There was a heavenly consultation. Long before human life as we know it existed, long before the earth was with form. God had desired that
the heavenly establishment would be replicated and humans would rule the earth with similar structure. Now whether that plan fell through or not is debate for another day. This neither negates nor nullifies the original intentions or purpose. God has a plan for you and it's a well thought out plan.

A woman can only fully understand who she is by understanding the components that constitute her being. We understand in genesis that God made us in His image. Now an image is not a look alike neither is it a semblance, an image is an exact reflection of one's self. On the day of creation God made himself expressed as human so in actual fact he made god and as He exist in triune so do we. In woman's understanding of self she must know that her physical body is just one of the many constituents that comprise to make self. In actuality woman consist of spirit, soul and body. A fulfilled woman is she who is one with all three components of her being. God doesn't exist as a separate entity he exists coherently as a trinity. Likewise our triune is in our

Who am I ?

spirit, soul and body. There must be a balance for us to function effectively in purpose. Let's look at these three components extensively.

WOMAN AND HER SPIRIT *(Pneuma)*
WOMAN AND HER SOUL *(Psyche)*
WOMAN AND HER BODY *(Soma)*

SPIRIT---SOUL----BODY. (INTER -CONNECTIVITY)

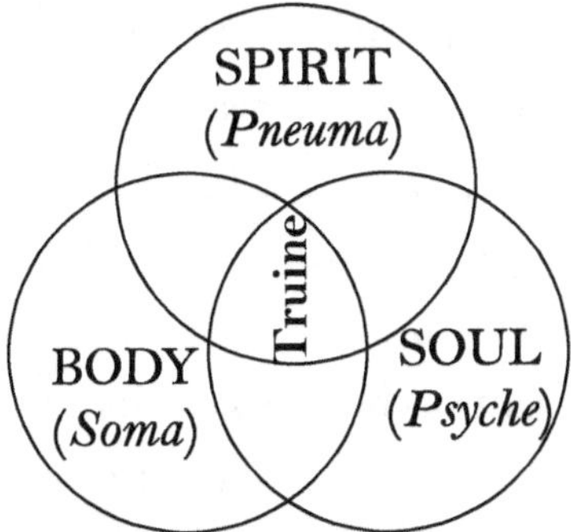

The inter-connectivity of the mind, body and Spirit has been dismissed by scientist as "quantum flap doodle" a concept popularized by physic Murray Gell Mann. But I'd rather lean towards leading physic, Sir Rudolf Peierls stance on its inter-connectivity and interpretation or knowledge of functionality on each component. Hear him,

'the premise that you can describe in terms of physics the whole functions of a human being ... including its knowledge, and its consciousness is untenable".

Who am I ?

We know for a fact that neither physics nor science for that matter has all the answers to knowledge of human existence or its total component.

WOMAN AND HER SPIRIT.

The complexity of the internal working of the human and their insatiable quest for point of equilibrium makes it impossible not to presume at the least that there has to be more to us than just what we see in time and space. We have to be much more than matter. People have said that we are spirits on a human journey and they wouldn't be far from the truth. Survivors of near death incidents narrate stories of out of body experiences with accounts that they were actually transported out of their bodies and viewed events and or operational procedures and resuscitating interventions carried out on them. People have even boldly claimed to have gone to the world beyond and come back with tales of the afterlife.

People have been quick to dispel these claims as mere hallucinations and typical of brain function as a results of huge rush of blood to the brain which is usual in cases of extreme trauma and escalated fatigue.

That might be a medical explanation, however we must

not be quick to brush this aside because even scientist know as we have stated earlier that science alone cannot explain everything. An account in the book Matthew popularly termed the transfiguration, Jesus was joined by both Moses and Elijah on a mountain been witnessed by three of Jesus' "inner circle" disciples and both prophets were long dead! Now how could they possibly have been connecting and
conversing with Jesus who was at the time officially human. His spirit had connected with theirs and the three held on a conversation uninterrupted. He had switched to another spiritual dimension and as such was able to connect with them.

If we as humans must connect on another dimension spiritually we must first acknowledge and activate our spiritual authority. The bible clearly states that God is a spirit and those that will worship him must do so in spirit and in truth. The spirit of humans must be alive to be able to connect with the supernatural through the help of one of the triune, God-the Holy Spirit. But what's the point, some may add. The point is that without the connection you cannot find the much desired balance or what we may term as oneness or total peace. To find yourself, you must find your spirit and get your oneness. Absence of which would result in a void resulting in disequilibrium or what I term "disquiet existence". That's why people all over the world try to ensure that that void is filled; now filling it up the right way and the more acceptable way is critical if a woman must reach her **"alpha existence".** You can only achieve so much with physical and or intellectual prowess, but with the assistance of the supernatural, your efforts are somewhat God-like. Your spirit is eternal, that means that your spirit never dies. It lives forever. Physical death cannot bring it to extinction.

It's worthy to note that religion cannot guarantee you that connection, neither can morality nor legality but a reliance and acceptance of an exclusive right of connection by your spirit with God's spirit and on His terms. Remember He is the creator of man and He was the one that put the spirit in man.

A woman that decides to pursue her spiritual reinvigoration is a powerful and wise woman. Mary, the mother of the messiah and Elisabeth, her cousin, experienced very robust spiritual occurrences, the former being personally visited by Gods angel Gabriel and was told that she was highly favoured. He also acknowledged that the Lord was with her. She wasn't religious but rather enjoyed a personal relationship with her spiritual father. Her spirit was in tune with her fathers. Religion hardly makes your spirituality genuine but relationship. Many religious people hardly make the bar for acceptable relationships because of the many hindrances and legalities that come with religion. That's why time and again Jesus spoke against the status quo of established religions of his time. He one time even boldly said that they taught their own traditions as tradition and teachings of God, a trend he greatly frowned upon.

For a woman to enjoy her spirituality with God she must rise above religion and strive deeply for relationship. The spirit mastered woman is the one who has the capacity for total and complete fulfillment. A wholesome spirit is a prerequisite for life's equilibrium for any woman whose desire is to enjoy oneness of self. Success can be subtle; many seemingly successful people take their own life out of a lack of fulfillment.

That's why the human spirit was made as the third and very important component of the human triune. It gives life, power and energy. It is specifically to connect to a supernatural and Spirit-God, to fill the void in your life and create the much needed calm for everyday living.

Who am I ?

The calmness and the comfort you get from the knowledge that you cannot have all the answers, you cannot solve all the problems and you cannot make all your problems and those of the world go away with a magic wand, after all you're still just human. Every woman must be in tune with her spirit she must awaken her spirit, she must feed, nurture and care for her spirit.

The spirit must never be left unattended. It's your weapon, it's your defense, and it's your access to purpose. Make that connection today.

WOMAN AND HER SOUL (Psyche)

INFLOW¡æ¡æ¡æ [   ] ¡æ¡æ¡æPERCEPTION

The second most profound component of the triune is the soul which is often referred to as the essence of the individual. The extent of the exaction of your soul is what would determine the height of your attainment of total fulfillment. While your spirit is necessary for balance, connectivity to God and hopefully a happily ever after in the afterlife, the soul's development is necessary for the attainment of purpose and all that life has in store for you. The soul is where perception is birth. It comprises your mind which includes your conscience, your will and your emotions. It forms your reasoning, your imaginations and memory. It is often described as link between your conscious and unconscious state. In your unconscious state, it's your dreams, imaginations and desires. In your conscious state it's your ideals, responses, attitudes, and intellect.

Because none of us is born with preconceived perceptions, ideals or attitudes, we cannot claim to be formed as a result of birth rather as a result of transferred, taught, learned ideals and norms that invariably shape our reactions, attitudes and responses. Everything you experience is information in your mind People that are constantly around hate often times reflect same because they have been exposed to hate overtime and have trained their subconscious to accept such emotions as normal and acceptable hence creating conscious reactions displaying hate tendencies. In "intuitive life coaching" its termed **Neuro Linguistic Programming (NLP).** Therefore it's safe to conclude that everything I have accepted as normal is what I have been exposed to and have conditioned myself through my subconscious mind as acceptable. In a nutshell I become what I constantly think . The most powerful weapon on earth is not any known ammunition rather

Who am I ?

it's the human mind. The human mind is capable of doing anything it thinks it can.

In Genesis, we read about a story of a group of people who imagined building a tower that would reach up to heaven. Unimaginable you think? Well, God didn't think so; in fact He was so convinced they could achieve it He personally had to do something about stopping them. The human mind is as potent as death itself. Everything on earth is as a result of the mind. Every invention that has been made and would ever be made would be as a result of someone's mind. Every expression be it of love, hate, sympathy, envy etc would all originate from the mind.

Most of the evil devises of all ages sprung from the mind of debased individuals, terrorism, racism, apartheid, injustice, ethnic cleansing, etc all begin in the mind and it would have to take much more than legislature, litigation, jail time, activism or fanatism to tackle it. It would have to take a mind
intervention to tackle it. Just as God intervened by interrupting their ambitious imagination and preventing them from speaking with one voice that's how mind interventions can be effective.

The woman who has mastered the power and use of her

mind would rule her world. The mind is large enough to receive as many information as you may be willing to give it. The more it gets the larger and more valuable the person gets. An exposed mind is a liberated soul. The bible says that it is the lack of knowledge that kills. Knowledge is for everyone that desires it.

Within five minutes conversations with anyone you can tell very easily how much that person has invested in their minds. Let's look at a popular story in the book of Daniel, the children of Israel knew that they had suffered for too long in captivity in Babylon, but interestingly, it was only the prophet Daniel who understood that their time in captivity ought to have elapsed. And he got that information through books. This prompted him to place a demand on God because of the knowledge he had.

A powerful woman is one who has the required knowledge to stay ahead of her game. For a long time women were made to believe that they could only function in the bedroom and kitchen, today we know that it's one of the oldest lies that's been told that it has begun to be generally accepted as truth. The reason we know its untrue is because today women have headed corporations, states and governments. Today women have gone to the moon, gone to space and flown fighter jets. Women, like their male counter parts can be and do anything they put their hearts and mind to.

Your mind must be opened up and one of the surest ways is through books. I try to make it a point of duty to read at least a book every month. Nelson Mandela while in incarceration at the notorious Robbin Island was quoted to have said how much reading and writing occupied his mind completely and how it would later guide his philosophy, his reactions and practically nearly every decision he made.

For a long time during the apartheid era in South Africa, political and black history books were banned because they understood that when you expose people to truths and especially history people begin to ask question and demand answers, answers I'm sure the apartheid government of South Africa were neither equipped nor prepared to answer. You want to find answers? read books, you want to get ahead?, read books, you want to know your rights and privileges? read books, you want to get the truth? read books. Just read books. Enrich your soul; it's your sure way to enhancing purpose.

WOMAN AND HER BODY.

The human body connotes the entire physical structure of a human being. The human body is the only legally authorized form for identification and recognition on earth. People have estimated the human body to cost from as low as 5cents to as much as 6trillion dollars, however we know that to put a monetary value on something as priceless as life is ludicrous and even hilarious. Even though the human body is made from dust, we aren't expected to treat it degradedly, the human body has been described as Gods abode and the best work of art, as such we are expected to treat it with respect. As a matter of fact the way we care for our bodies shows how much we respect ourselves and God. The human body unlike the soul and spirit is mortal, it is flesh and weak. It has its own agendas and desires which are more often than not contrary to your life's purpose. The body comes with one main agenda that is to pleasure itself. While it isn't entirely wrong to want to pleasure our bodies we must know how to put it in check so it doesn't run riot and consume our purpose, and it should not be by physically depriving it of things that would ordinary be good for it but rather subject it to the ruler ship of your soul and spirit.

The female body is a beautiful creation and it must be taken care of. Women must learn how to treat their bodies to regular bouts of pampering and care, the use of bathing soaps, fragrances, scents, beauty herbs and oils should be encouraged. I've met with several women who tell me that they feel guilty and very vain when they engage in exercises like these. And I'm almost always quick to point out that Jesus didn't frown when Mary Magdalene poured very expensive scents upon His feet and wiped it with her hair and even rebuked those who felt it was totally unnecessary and wasteful.

We must never feel ashamed or apologetic in wanting to care for our bodies, we owe no one excuses for the care we give our bodies. It is a disservice to you. Marianne Williamson speaks so eloquently in this regard and it should be your watchword when the temptation to feel guilty about pampering your body comes to you.

"… we ask ourselves who am I to be brilliant, gorgeous, talented, fabulous? Actually, who are you not to be? You are a child of God…we are all meant to shine, as children do." Scents have been used since ancient times and even dates to as far back as 4th century BC. We read in Esther how she spent 6 months bathing in oil and myrrh and additional 6 months in sweet odors and other things for the purification of the women just to be able to stand before the king!

"Enjoy your feminity, enjoy your beauty, there is beauty in every colour, no one particular race or tribe has the exclusive right to beauty. We are all wonderfully made and beautifully sculptured, including you ".

We should not be quick to

Who am I ?

forget the simple lessons on hygiene we learnt in elementary school; they remain true
throughout our lifetime. Our general appearance must reflect cleanliness and beauty from our heads to our toes. Care for your bodies and every part of it. You are the custodian of the body handed over to you for life and you must treat it with dignity and respect.
Enjoy your femininity, enjoy your beauty, there is beauty in every colour, no one particular race or tribe has the exclusive right to beauty. We are all wonderfully made and beautifully sculptured, including you. Take advantage of every opportunity to make yourself look and feel pretty. Care about how you look every day, how you dress, what you wear, what you eat, how you eat what you eat. Every day keep an appointment with your body.

There are 5 do and 5 dot's in treating your bodies.
FIVE DOS
- Beautify it
- Nature it
- Respect it
- Honuor it
- Feed it
FIVE DON'TS
- Don't misuse it,
- Don't abuse it,
- Don't deprive it,
- Don't ignore it
- Don't deface it.

So woman go ahead and love YOU totally. You are God's master plan. The very last link in God's creation. You are made in the image and similitude of God for a particular purpose which is for the benefit of mankind. Never forget for a moment who you are. Refuse to be defined on anyone terms because you are female rather choose to be defined by your God given purpose.

As you read on it is my belief that you would discover purpose and have a complete and holistic definition of who you really are!

WORKBOOK
CHAPTER ONE

As we have seen in the first chapter, in defining who we are; we must first understand who we are as God sees us, this is usually in relation to our purpose or assignment.

So I would like you to list out some of the ways God sees you, you can use Psalm 139 as a guide.

____

____

____

____

____

____

Now list out the way you see yourself.

____

____

____

____

____

____

Who am I ?

How are you as a woman different from a man?

How are you as a woman similar to a man?

So how are your strengths unique?

Do you see yourself as a competitor or a collaborator?
List the reasons for either answer that you give.

Has the book helped you with clarifying? Explain.

The three components in our definition of self.
Spirit, soul and body.
How can you describe your spirituality?

What steps are you taking to ensure that your spirit is not neglected?

____

____

____

____

____

____

____

____

____

How does your spirit connect with the Holy Spirit to access spiritual things, seeing that a spiritual woman is a strong woman?

____

____

____

____

____

____

What steps are you going to take to ensure that you feed your mind so that you master your emotion?

____

____

____

____

____

____

____

____

What type of books do you think you need to help boost your self-esteem / self-worth?

____

____

____

____

____

____

Do you feel guilty when you pamper your body?

____

____

____

If you answered yes, why do you think you do?

____

____

____

____

Why do you think you should not?

____

____

____

____

____

____

How has the book helped you in understanding the importance of caring for your bodies and not feeling guilty?

____

____

____

____

____

____

____

____

Do you think God cares about how you care for yourself?

____

____

____

____

____

____

____

How can you care for your bodies?

How are you unique?

Chapter

2

We are daddy's little girls and
we can do anything and be
anything because daddy's
there by our side.

WHOSE I AM

Daddy And His Little Girls.

*"Behold I've engraved you upon the palms of
my hands...." Isaiah 49:16*

Big Strong Arms.

No one can hurt a little girl where her father is and that's a fact. His presence by her side gives her a calm assurance and this she knows quite well. My little girl Juanita loves her dad very much and believe me it's mutual. I noticed every time her dad came back home she would begin to jumble things all around the house and stare at me defiantly almost daring me to challenge her if I could. It always makes me laugh. My baby girl has a big daddy alright, all 6ft plus of him.

We are usually that way when we know who's got our back. It's like insurance against any eventualities. We are daddy's little girls and we can dance around, do anything, be anything and climb the highest mountain because daddy's right there by our side. God compares His affection for us over and above a mother's love. Trust me coming from a mother that's a big thing!

His love for us has no boundaries, it's without restrictions and its unconditional meaning that nothing we can ever do will influence his love negatively or positively. It's a fathers love for his daughter, no matter how bruised, broken, dysfunctional, abused, rejected, bowed down you may think you are

His plans are to do you good all the days of your life. Just like our earthly fathers, our heavenly father desires the best for us. He asks which among us would their child ask for bread and

would give him a stone? I can't think of any. Nothing gladdens a father's heart than to see his children laugh and be happy. It's been said that a parent is as happy as his saddest child and nothing can be truer than that. When a child hurts, a parent hurts and it's the same with our heavenly father. He's desirous for us to live happy and fulfilled lives, one with purpose.

The surest way to live a life of purpose is to ensure our eyes stay focus on the finish line. What you might call: keeping your eyes on the ball Staying focus on the things that really matter. You achieve this by looking ahead and resisting ferociously the temptation to look back. Every sprinter knows the implication of looking back in a race. That one singular action could cost the sprinter the ultimate prize and even the entire race.

We have to learn to live forward by effectively dealing with the past. Until we learn how to deal with the past we may never really be on the part of purpose. The reason is because your past is at constant loggerheads with your journey forward. I'll show you how to deal with it.

<u>*Whose I am*</u>

DEALING WITH THE PAST.

Dealing with the past can be daunting. Every single day of our lives we are constantly reminded of our past failures and the many decisions, actions and inactions we took or failed to take that has kept us in the situation we are now, we are continually reminded of the many reasons why we shouldn't be permitted to go forward. The past hangs as an albatross, we're torn between moving forward despite our past baggage and we look back trying to figure out how things could have turned out differently and we end up in limbo.

But we are strongly advised by the Apostle Paul to put the past behind us. The reason is because too much concentration on the past incapacitates our ability to forge forward towards purpose, no one gets ahead looking back.

George Washington advised that we should not look back unless it is to derive useful lessons from past errors and for the purpose of profiting by dearly bought experience.

"God can use anyone at anytime for anything without recourse to their past because He is God"

You have to constantly remind yourself who you are and the enviable position God has placed you. So anytime you are tempted to look back at all your past failures and shortcomings be quick to look at the future and all its limitless possibilities. Every day brings with it new hopes, new adventures, new opportunities. Nobody with a great and successful story today doesn't have some sordid past to compliment it, so do yourself a favour and forget the past. Everybody's got a story and believe me it's not pretty!

I remember the story of the woman who was a member of a local church cell group who was complaining about how she
couldn't possibly be used by God because according to her she had done some very heinous things in her past and she was confiding in the prayer cell leader but the response from her cell leader shocked her even more.

She said 'if I told you mine you'd shudder,"

Everyone has a story honey so it's best you move on and don't dignify your past with a rear view mirror. There's nothing new under the sun.

Someone else has been there, done that and bought a t-shirt to prove it; but the reason you are unaware of their past is because they have chosen to let it go and make the best of a situation they have no power to undo. Let's learn like the apostle Paul to put the past where it belongs- behind us.

"This one thing I do forgetting those things that are behind, I press on towards the prize of the higher calling of Christ Jesus" phil 3:13

> *"It's a fathers love for his daughter, no matter how bruised, broken, dysfunctional, abused, bowed down you may think you are"*

The past must remain in the past because it is history! God can use anyone at anytime for anything without recourse to your past because His God.

God can use anyone, he can take a ruddy shepherd boy and make him king. He can take a prison boy and make him prime minister; he can take an orphaned slave girl and make her queen. He can take a young alien widow and make her a married woman of influence. He surely can use you woman despite your past.

When next the past comes to hunt you ask yourself these three questions with the corresponding answers

Can I change it? No I can't

Whose I am

Should I make up for it? Yes I should
Can I make up for it? Yes I can

 And then begin to take the necessary steps to make up for it through a clearly defined plan which may be with or without the assistance of a qualified expert trained to handle such cases but we know that the ultimate healer of past guiltiness is God and our self determination to ensure that we overcome our past. Everybody can take those constructive correctional steps to forgetting their past and forging ahead. Every new day is an opportunity to begin again, let your new day be today as you're reading this book.

I do a bit of volunteering in my local community with street kids and vulnerable women and I've met with women who have transformed their lives and begin doing awesome things largely because they allowed themselves to be touched by a loving father. The second He touches you, His love envelopes your total being and leads you towards your first step to learning to love again.

The first step starts with learning to forgive yourself and giving yourself the permission to love yourself. God expects us to love ourselves that's why he urges us to love others as we love ourselves, not more or less than the way we love ourselves. That feeling of deflatedness isn't peculiar to you, it's universal and cuts across women of different strata, tribe and creed. A human being comes with a lot of baggage and it's intentional. We would cease to be human without the imperfections. We must consciously and constantly teach ourselves how to love

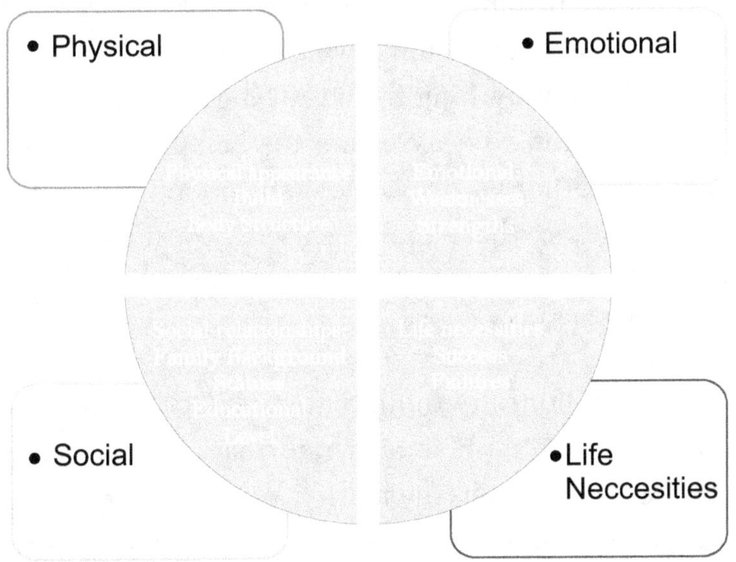

PHYSICAL

Your physical appearance is carefully thought out. By far the most detailed person I know is God. If he made you then you better believe it that He thought it through. Gods attention to detail is legendary, in the construction of Noah's Arch, we read how He gave specific instructions in the type, quantity, quality and measurement of every single material to be used in its construction and even the precise number and sex of each animal permitted to come into the arch. Everything must be carried out according to plan.

Again, every time a terbanacle was to be constructed in His honour, the builders weren't left to their discretion nor expertise, they would have to follow laid down instructions, everything from the length to the breath of materials must be according to plan. God wouldn't have it any other way. Specific instructions were given to the builders, what should be used, how it should be used and what manner it should be administered. It mattered to Him.

Now do you honestly think that same God could have gotten it wrong with your own formation? Truth is you don't have a choice in the matter, your purpose was thought out and your expression must of a necessity be tailor made to execute your assignment. Very often, people often tend to limit predestination only in terms of a person's call or purpose and often overlook the bearer of that purpose. The bearer is as important to the call as his/her assignment and you better believe that you are tailored made for that assignment. God is yet to make an error. Your physical appearance, race,

colour, gender, and every attribute that you possess is in line with Gods plan for your assignment.
Lots of women struggle with accepting their physical appearance and some even go to extreme measures to ensure that they get the bodies of their dreams. The cosmetic surgery industry is a multibillion dollar one and cosmetics surgeons are one of, if not, the most highly paid doctors in the
world.

Make no mistake; I don't take for granted the tremendously destabilizing and demoralizing effect one gets from feelings of inadequateness especially as it concerns women. I've also had to struggle with it too, in fact I've hardly met any woman or man for that matter who hasn't struggled with it one time or the other. But what we are trying to solve physically is incapable of being cured physically.

We have let the world define physical beauty with images that are very far from reality. Most of us are literally chasing shadows. Even people who turn to cosmetic surgery to achieve this beauty never achieve it because it's nonexistent. Beauty is relative and indeed a very personal thing.

The sooner you get it that your physical appearance is

just about right for your purpose, the better for you. You're potter made for your assignment. Your appearance, structure, build is all part of God's plan to fit into His purpose for you. Any distortions qualifies you for someone else assignment. Learn to love and appreciate the way you are. It's part of God's overall plan.

For years I struggled with accepting my physical appearance. I'd always wanted a bit more height and more curves like every other woman until I let God teach me how to appreciate his perfect and complete work in perfect in me . God loves you the way you were made. Love yourself and all you physical attributes! It's part of the plan.

> *"Your emotional control comes from a mastery of your strengths and not an absence of weakness"*

EMOTIONAL: Strengths & Weaknesses.

Women are often called emotional creatures with emotions running riot all over the place. However, the women who understand the science of emotional mastery rise above the rest. Your emotional control comes from a mastery of your strengths and not an absence of weakness. People that enjoy emotional control are not people without weaknesses, never let that sleek exterior fool you, there's not a single human being without a weakness. The best way is to commit it to God and refuse to let it deny of delay you of your life's purpose.

I had a friend in college who had high levels of stage freight and equally very timid and she approached me one day and asked me how I could just walk up boldly to people and convey a message or just ask their attention

 And she asked me. "Winnie, how do I overcome my timidity and be just like you?"

I laughed to that and responded "Me! I'm scared stiff of approaching people, I'm just like you but I don't let it stop me, I just say a brief prayer and go for it, there's really no trick nor any one fast and hard rule to it. Everyone has varying degrees of stage freight but the ones who go out there with their message in spite of their freight are the ones called bold, you too can be bold"

I remembered her smile and her response.

"Yeah right, easier said than done, my dear"

Today she's one of the finest speakers I've heard and she speaks on wellness and fitness. She must have learnt something.

Whose I am

46

Start today to determine that your weaknesses would no longer define what or who you will see, approach or do. So go ahead, let your strengths make up for your weakness.

You must learn to love your strengths; they are given to us to help us solve the puzzle of our purpose. Strengths lead us to our purpose. These strengths must be harnessed because if left fallow, they become redundant. They must be used to your advantage and must be applied in your pursuit of purpose.

These are a list of some of the strengths and weaknesses that either make or mar YOU in achieving purpose.

Differentiating Weakness from Bad Habits.
The temptation to mistake a weakness for a bad habit is very probable. A weakness which is usually innate deals with ones character but a habit on the other hand is usually formed overtime and often done repeatedly and most times without thinking, if it's a bad action it is termed as bad. These habits are cultivated overtime.

STRENGTHS	WEAKNESSES
Perseverance	Timidity
Enthusiasm	Rude
Devotion	Pessimistic
Loyalty	Self centered
Tolerance	Naïve
Trustworthiness	stand-offish
Respectful	Aggressive
Generous	Myopic
Inspiring	Fearful
Lively	Obstructive
Persuasive	Inhibited
Idealistic	Dull
Determination	Uninspiring
Independence	Shallow
Tactful	Impatient
Honest	Uncaring
Patient	Inconsiderate
Ambitious	Blunt
Optimistic	Harsh
Observant	Moody
Caring	Reckless
Considerate	Complaining

While weaknesses and bad habits are different, they can both keep us from achieving our purpose for different reasons. A bad habit like procrastination and a weakness like timidity can keep you away from taking opportunities but for different reasons; the one who procrastinated is neither prepared nor aware of an opportunity and the other's lack of courage to take advantage of opportunities prevents her from attaining it. One out of a bad habit and the other out of a weakness. So start now to cultivate habits and work on those weaknesses that are preventing you from pursing purpose

SOCIAL.

You must learn to love your relationships, family and friends. The reason you must learn to love your family is because your family is your first experience of unconditional love. Your earthly mother and father love you not because of anything you have earned but just because you are theirs. I have two kids and I can tell you emphatically that they don't have to say or do anything for me to love them. My

"You were born to the right folks and the right family. God knew that the experiences needed to mould you for your assignment needed to be among the people you were born into"

love for them is unconditional. That relationship shows you at such an early age an earthly example of a heavenly expression of love.

Even as much as God gives us freewill, God didn't give us a choice in the family we are born into. That choice remains His exclusive right. So rest assured, you were born to the right folks and the right family. learn to love your family inspite of all the craziness and chaos. God knew that the experiences needed to mould you for your assignment needed to be among the people you were born into.

You may not always agree with your folks but they mean well and just like God, it may be a bit difficult understanding the reasons behind the things that he does but in the end it all seems to fall in place. Love your family and your background, it's part of the plan. Remember that your family and background doesn't define you it only moulds you.

I've known some of the finest and most successful people on earth who had absolutely nothing and were from very humble backgrounds with crazy and messed up families. I met a young man named Israel recently at an event organized for volunteers and he shared one of the most inspiring stories I had heard. He narrated to the young volunteers how he was born in abject poverty, resided in the slums and shared a room with his mother and four other siblings but was able to earn an international degree and has met with the Queen of England. He remarked how his background helped mould him into the man he is today.

Because of his inspiring story he's helping other inner-city kids believe in themselves, shun violence and break stereotypes. Jesus was the son of a carpenter and born in a manger! He turned out okay! So love your family and your background, it's part of Gods plan.

RELATIONSHIPS.

Learn to love your relationships, they'll teach you life's lessons: loyalty, betrayal, sacrifice, selfishness, wisdom, folly and everything in between. Relationships help you appreciate life as it really is. I've seen people change from faithful friend to betrayer in an instant. They are just being who they are and trust me it's not about you. If you understand this then you have mastered one of life's greatest lessons.- the fickleness of people!

A variation from this norm is in the minority and it has absolutely nothing to do with the things you did or didn't do to them in the relationship. They just happen to be human that's all.

Guess what?, while Jesus was on earth to fufuil his assignment, his right hand man, one of this very own hand chosen apostle led a team of men to betray him and have him crucified. That

> *To those of us who are on the partway of success and in hot pursuit of purpose; failure is inevitable but we must understand failure for what it is. It is the required catalyst for transformation*

was over 2000 years ago. nothing much has changed since then. Humans are humans and they would continue
to be. Just learn from whatever experience and move on.

FAILURES.

Never be afraid of failing, for one it means you have ventured something and it didn't work. Henry ford said it's just an opportunity to begin again more intelligently. Your venturing into something and failing is actually success in disguise because you have learnt something new from that failed attempt.

When Thomas Edison was asked by a reporter how it felt to fail 1000 times in his attempts at inventing the light bulb, he responded " I didn't fail 1,000 times ,the light bulb was an invention with a 1000 steps" it's all about perception. How can I eventually know my purpose and create my niche if I have never failed at something. The failure is a clear indication that you need to retrace, redirect, re-strategize or refocus your resources in some other direction.

If Thomas Edison had given up because he considered himself a failure at the 999th time, he most certainly wouldn't have been the inventor of the light bulb because the light bulb would still be invented.

People, who don't venture anything, don't do anything, don't try anything, may think that they never get to fail but they do fail at the most important thing –LIFE. They never get to experience life. To fail is not the bad part but staying at the
point of failure is the bad part. Every great man or woman has had their fair share of failure. Hear what legendary American basketballer, Michael Jordan said about failing, "I've missed more than 9000 shots in my career. 26times I've been trusted to take the games winning shot…and missed. I've failed over and over and over again in my life. That's why I succeed."

To those of us who are on the partway of success and in

hot pursuit of purpose; failure is inevitable but we must understand failure for what it is. It is the required catalyst for transformation. It is meant to make us stronger and wiser. So don't shy away from failure. It's part of the plan, it gives you wisdom and experience.

SUCCESS.

"Seeth a man diligent in his work, he would stand before kings and not mere men" Proverbs 22:29

Success is a reward for hard work.
Success is not coincidental; I constantly remind my team members that success never stumbles on anyone. It's a series of deliberate and conscious series of activities and events that creates a desired result. I've never heard of any successful person who says 'Oh! I don't know how success came to me, I wasn't even expecting it' that's because it's a series of calculated activities and events. Now you may have opportunities here and there, connections here and there but
success comes about because those opportunities were utilized to multiply returns.

It's important to enjoy and celebrate your successes but don't get carried away that you become complacent. You must not rest on your oars of success. There are better ways of doing things. Innovations are coming at the speed of light. The world is evolving daily. So succeeding and remaining on the same spot is complacent.

We read a story in the bible of the transfiguration, where Elijah and Moses appeared unto Jesus at Mount Olives in the presence of the apostles and the apostles suggested that they remain there and build terbanacles for three. But Jesus had bigger plans i.e. to save the world. He couldn't be talked into staying there and celebrating his very distinguished guests. He had a larger goal which must be attained.

What if he had agreed with them to remain there and keep gloating over their small feat. He wouldn't have fulfilled the greatest assignment of all time. Don't be comfortable with that success remember there's a bigger goal!

So here's the summation of it all. Love your physical appearance, it's part of God's plan for your assignment. Love your strengths it propels you towards purpose. Downplay your weaknesses, they're there to remind us we human after all.

Learn from your failures, it's what makes you wiser. Enjoy your successes; it's your reward for hard work.

Love your family/background it's what has shaped you to be you.

Love your relationships they've taught you life's lessons-betrayal, friendship, loyalty, love(conditional and unconditional) and best of all, Love yourself, you were worth dying for.

"for God so loved the world that he gave His only begotten Son that whosoever believes in Him should not die but have everlasting life" John 3:16

WORKBOOK
CHAPTER TWO

As we have seen in the second chapter, finding purpose has
a lot with knowing whose you are, dealing with your past
and also learning to love yourself totally – physically,
emotionally, socially and all that life throws at you.
So I would like you to list out some of the ways you feel
God acts as your daddy
.

____

____

____

____

____

____

____

____

____

____

Do you feel deserving of anyone's love and protection?
Express your reasons for any answer you have given.

How has the book helped in reassuring you of God's love?

Read Isaiah 49:16

____

____

____

____

____

Dealing with your past.
Can you list some of the incidents that keeps recurring in your mind causing you to ruminate and refer to your past?

____

____

____

____

____

____

____

____

Now can you honestly undo any of the listed incidents?

____

____

____

____

If you cannot, it is important that you focus on any three of the following actions listed below as it relates to your situation.

1. Forgive myself and move on
2. Reconcile with myself, my hurt, my pain and let go.
3. Take action and get help- Counseling & Therapy

   Support groups

   Activity tracking.

   Coaching.

Learning to love yourself.
Physical.
What is it about you physically that you love the most?

____

____

____

____

____

____

What is it about you physically that you do not appreciate.
Read psalm 139.

____

____

____

____

____

Read what is written below carefully and repeat it to
yourself until you get it.
 I am BEAUTIFUL, BEAUTIFUL, and BEAUTIFUL. My
PURPOSE preceded my formation. My physique and
everything about me is tailor made for my assignment. It's
all part of the plan.
Re write it below as an affirmation.

____

____

____

____

____

Can you look at yourself in the mirror and begin to see

Whose I am

yourself just as beautiful as you truly are.

____

____

____

Emotional.
Don't fret about this list, everybody has one weakness or the other so don't be afraid to list them. This is the first step in addressing those weaknesses. Can you list those weakness that are hindering you from moving forward and pursuing your goals?

____

____

____

____

____

____

____

____

____

Can you list your strengths that you feel would help you in achieving your goals?

____

____

____

____

____

____

____

Can you list out some of the ways you can harness your strengths and downplay your weaknesses to ensure you fulfill purpose?

____

____

____

____

____

____

____

Social.

Do you consider yourself to be ashamed of your

background?

____

____

Has the book helped you in understanding the need not to?

____

____

____

Now that you have thought through all those experiences

growing up with your friends and family can you list out

some of the lessons those experiences have taught you in

life and how they would/have helped shape your decisions

in life?

____

____

____

____

____

____

____

____

____

____

____

Can you also list some of the things your past relationships have taught you, even though they were very painful or otherwise at the time?

____

____

____

____

____

____

Can you also list some of the things your past failures have taught you?

What would you do differently with what you know now?

____

____

____

____

____

____

Can you also list some of the things your past successes have taught you?

____

____

____

____

____

____

____

____

Can you list some of the biggest take-aways this chapter
has taught you as an individual and as a woman?

____

____

____

____

____

____

____

____

____

____

Chapter

3

"An Unemployed Existence is a
Worse Negation of Life Than
Death Itself."

Jose Gasset

MY PURPOSE,
MY PASSION,
MY DRIVE.

"The purpose of life is a life of purpose"
Robert byme.

Nothing is created for the sake of creation. Everything created is made with a purpose in mind. Much as there exist very convincing arguments for the big bang theory as the origin of life, I would rather differ strongly. The structure and complexity of the world and its inhabitants tend to suggest and appeal at least to my mind of a more deliberate, intentional and preplanned thought to life's origin and existence. In my opinion the big bang theory just doesn't cut it.

Everything has a reason to be made. Notice I said everything that is inclusive of manmade items- the gas cooker enables cooking, the dish washer washes dishware, the elevator eases flight, the refrigerator cools and preserves e.t.c. Now all these are manmade inventions and each without a purpose so what makes you think you were made to satisfy nothing and no one. If there wasn't a need you wouldn't be made.

If men could sit down, conceptualize and invent something to meet a specific need you'd better believe that the creator of man carried out precisely the same process. I had said earlier that a consultation was carried out by the **God-head** to replicate heavenly rulership and authority on earth for a generic purpose. Gods original intent and purpose for man was to dominate, rule and

reign as kings and Queens on this earth.
However each of us is to have individual and specific assignments reigning as kings and queens in that assignment.

These assignments are neither garlanded with masculine nor feminine undertone but are given according to specific requirements. In other words, I am not given a particular assignment because I'm female but rather am given an assignment because I'm human and there is a need for that purpose which I have been equipped to fulfill. Every human on earth have both generic and individual purposes. Generically, we all were to be fruitful, to multiply, replenish, subdue and dominate the earth. It's important to chip here that this proclamation was for the human species, that is whether male or female.

The human species was given the authority to dominate the earth but certainly not each other. Many people erroneously think that the male were commanded by God to dominate their female counterparts but they have been economical with the truth. They usually cite a popular scripture in Ephesians 6, were the wife was told to be submissive to her husband. But what they have failed to realize is that the woman wasn't instructed to be submissive to everyman but rather to be submissive to her own husband and the reason even isn't sexist but rather for orderliness and structure in a family unit. Man ie male and female were both given the authority by God to rule, dominate, subdue the earth, its elements, circumstances and situations by our divinity and not each other. The blessing and authority was given to the human race.

Let's critically look at each of the authorities given to man at the beginning of creation because our understanding of each of these terms would help us appreciate our triumphant predestination as a human beign and co-creator with God.

As a woman, you are called to be fruitful not only in terms of procreation but you were made to be fruitful in all areas of your life, in your business, career, finance, relationship and the likes. The results in your life were not to be restricted to only one outcome but multiple outcomes. The woman's life is one destined for multiple satisfactions.

My Purpose, My Passion, My Drive.

As a woman, you are born with innate multiplicity abilities. A life with limitless possibilities. Our result and performance in life were to only be restricted by the extent of our individual purpose and not our race or gender.

> *"Our result and performance in life were to only be restricted by the extent of our individual purpose and not our race or gender."*

While the Javan and Sumatran rhino are critically endangered and many more animals like the cape lion, North African elephant and gazelles are all extinct, the human race of which we belong can't go extinct because of our replenishing characteristics. We have the characteristics to reinvent and replenish ourselves.

After creation, the only pronouncement given to the human race exclusively was that of domination. Of all of God's creations, we are the only ones with the authority to dominate and subdue. It's who we were made to be. Whatever we have been called to do, first as a human being and as a woman, we must understand that we are structured with a mandate and authority to subdue and rule over circumstances, situation, finances, earthly elements in our favour to ensure the establishment of purpose.

My Purpose, My Passion, My Drive.

In our quest to fully understand the power of our potential as it relates to our purpose we can look at a very little seed like the mustard seed. Its understanding would help drive home some cogent truths about purpose and how it relates to our potential.

LESSONS FROM THE MUSTARD SEED.

Everything begins with a seed. Human life begins with a seed but it doesn't remain in that state for a long time. It evolves to its full potential through the process of time. Now the small black mustard seed is about 1/20th of an inch in size but it has the ability to grow up to 3.7 meters or
double the size of an average man, 12ft in height. That's amazing! This illustrates something which develops rapidly from small beginnings. Something so small developing into something of gigantic proportion.

How can this be? How can something so small get to be so big? Just doesn't add up, but that's the beauty and magnanimity of God. It was God who put such powerful potential into this seed. Often times it is very tempting to feel very small and incapable of doing great things, however we must never forget that the same God who gives such potential to this very tiny seed can do the same for you.

My Purpose, My Passion, My Drive.

He puts the potential in everything at the formative stage. The ability to be all it can be is already resided within self as little as it arrives. A baby already has it in him or her to become a man or a woman but only needs the much required time for processing. The baby already possesses the prerequisite for the attainment of purpose and this innate deposit or potential is what gears you to passion and ultimately purpose.

I get asked all the time so how do I know if I am living my purpose? And I tell them you don't struggle with purpose. You know immediately, it becomes as easy as reciting the alphabets. Purpose becomes you. Purpose finds you just as you find it.

Oprah Winfrey often tells of how she loved to talk a lot as a little girl and her grandmother's friend almost always referring to her love for talking every time they crossed paths at her new Baptist church. Today, until her retirement in 2012 she was America's number one talk show host.

Your purpose always finds you and no matter how long you run or how far you go, life leaves little clues along the way as to what your assignment is.

My Purpose, My Passion, My Drive.

Your purpose always finds you and no matter how long you run or how far you go, life leaves little clues along the way as to what your assignment is. For some it's as glaring as a little girl that sings and angels come down, to a little child whose inquisitive nature prompts her to want to invent little things. Or the little child who gets mad when she sees injustice and demands that there's retribution. The clues are all around you.

This brings us to the number one determiner or pointer to purpose- YOUR PASSION- it is the one sure clue as to what your assignment is. Whichever way it is, purpose finds you and its beguiled in your passion.

PASSION.

Every gift that you possess is an indication of where your purpose resides. Recognizing your gifts and talents is one of the surest ways to a happy and fulfilling life because it's what you were born to do.

The illustration of a fish in water is very apt in this analogy. A fish was born to swim so if you take a fish and put it in an environment of water, its innate skills of swimming comes to bear, it doesn't need any external

nor remote assistance to swim, it just does what it was born to do. It swims. But when you take that same fish and
put it on dry land it loses its star factor and gaps, it seems like it's an underachiever, yet nothing has really changed with the structure of that fish. The fish erroneously concludes that it's no good and it keeps struggling, getting frustrated and would ultimately die not because it didn't have it in it to succeed but because it didn't realize that it was made to swim and water is the best place for that skill to birth.

Using an inanimate object like the hammer is another typical example. The hammer can be made to perform several functions for which it wasn't made for. It can be used to hit things in place. You could even use it to pound bricks and further grind granular objects to finer substances. But in all of these functions the hammer doesn't seem to perform optimally, infact in some cases its performance can be described as lack luster especially when it is used to break hard concrete. It almost seems to take forever trying to do a simple task.

And that has absolutely nothing to do with either the hammer or the tasks but rather a misuse of the hammer. The hammer wasn't built for that. But when a hammer meets a nail, its performance is apt because function meets purpose. Its constituent parts comprises of the gifts that gives clues as to what its best suited to solve.

All our gifts are the little puzzles and clues to where our passion lies. It's a dangerous thing not to be nsync with purpose and unable to utilize your gifts or talents judiciously.

A famous story told by Jesus on talents in the book of Matthew is an all time winner in the explanation and defense of the fact that no one is without a gift or talent. He tells the story of the "good man" of a house going away on a far journey and giving talents to everyone in his household and it is indicative of how gifts play a pivotal role in our purpose.

Every purpose and assignment has a grace and when you operate outside your assignment and purpose, you work in disfavor and perpetual labour.

We are told that he gave five talents to one, to another he gave two and the last he gave one talent.

The story indicates some very vital points about gifts and talents: The first being that it is given to everyone and freely given. It doesn't come at a price; neither do you

My Purpose, My Passion, My Drive.

have to do anything to earn it.
Secondly, it is not uniform, similar or generic. It is given in accordance to needs, ability, purpose or calling.
Thirdly, you would be accountable for it. However way you have used it your talents will be accounted for.
Fourth, it has a multiplying effect.
Fifth, it is indestructible, you cannot destroy it, it may be left fallow for years but it remains.
And lastly, It is recyclable.

Now it is important to note here that while the gifts and callings of God are without repentance, it can be given to someone else if it remains redundant. God wouldn't take the gift back to Himself, however He could very well give it to someone who would make mighty use of it, and he can use anyone and anything so be mindful what you do with that God given gift.

There are many dissatisfied women all over the world because they are in areas and places where they cannot make best use of their talents. Most people end up getting jobs where they are paid to do what they loath making everyday like a chore with no motivation or desire to start the day.

That discomfort is an indication that you are in the wrong place. You don't quite fit because like it or not

My Purpose, My Passion, My Drive.

there are people right there who seem to having a ball in the place you describe as a hell hole.

Every purpose and assignment has a grace and when you operate outside your assignment or purpose you work in
disfavor and perpetual labour.

A friend of mine once confided in me and said he tried his hands on so many things until he gave it all up and pursued his passion for music. Today he runs a music club for young kids gifted in music to help them start early and to enjoy their God given talents.

Every purpose has a grace and until we find it and operate in it the struggle never ends.

FINDING PURPOSE:

By far the most asked question I get is "Winnie how do I find my purpose?"

That's why I have dedicated this aspect of the book to helping you out. It's also more elaborate in the workbook. These questions would help you on your pursuit of purpose:

1.   What do you enjoy doing
         (list top 3 in order of preference)
2.   What one thing would you do for free?
3.   What do you love to talk about?
4.   What are your values?
5.   What can you not ignore?

<u>My Purpose, My Passion, My Drive.</u>

6.   What can you invest your last money on?
7.   What inspires you and why?
8.   What problems do you constantly find
        people asking you to solve
9.   What would you teach for free?
10.   What matters to you most?
11.   What causes could you live for?
12.   What causes could you die for?
13.   If your life were to end today what would be you
        biggest regret?
14.   What would be your biggest joy?
13.   Who are you usually drawn to?
14.   Describe yourself in one word?
15.   What character do you struggle the most with?
16.   What character do you struggle the least with
17.   How do your friends describe you?
18.   How does your family describe you?
19.   How do your children describe you?
20.   How do your colleagues describe you?
21.   How does your boss describe you?
22.   How do your subordinates describe you?
25.   Would you describe yourself as an initiator,
        follower or loner?
26.   Do you see you self as an introvert or extrovert?

These questions are carefully thought out to enable the
seeker get an understanding of your obvious strength;
your hidden strength; your passion and perception and
the problem you are best suited to solve. Through my
years of life coaching and counseling, I've been able to

My Purpose, My Passion, My Drive.

help people identify these attributes; so they could begin to live purposely. You too can.

While appreciating your honesty in finding meaning to your life and goals, it's important to note that talent is never enough there are several unfulfilled women with tremendous talent.

Your gifts would make a way for you but to stay and remain relevant in the room would require a whole lot more than talent, it's your drive or what many would term "staying

PASSION ⇨ ⇨ ⇨ **DRIVE** ⇨ ⇨ ⇨ **PURPOSE**

DETERMINATION
DILIGENCE
ENTHUSIASM
INTEGRITY
KNOWLEDGE

Like we had said earlier, your drive is the determiner of your length or duration from passion to purpose. Your pursuit of purpose is your drive and it varies for everyone. Your drive is based upon the fundamental trenches of determination, diligence, integrity, enthusiasm and knowledge.

In order to live your purpose you must cultivate determination and perseverance. it's a long, hard road to purpose but finding it is the most rewarding feeling you would ever experience. It's very easy to take the simple route and live life unintentionally. It doesn't take any effort to give up at anything; it is by far the easiest of things to do. Your determination or your staying power would give you the necessary antidote for whatever life throws your way on your journey to your assignment.

Albert Einstein once said that "it's not that I'm so smart, it's just that I stay with problems longer."

If you are determined to take the necessary little steps today, you would eventually get there tomorrow. Start now to take
those little steps. Cut down on those things that are taking you away from purpose and spend more time on those things that facilitate purpose.

Hear what British billionaire and entrepreneur, Richard Branson has to say on perseverance and determination, "the ability to tap into your determination and grit is not just an innate skill. You can teach yourself to get up every day and try to keep a new business going despite long odds, partly by structuring your life, make sure you are working towards your larger goals."
You have to settle it in your mind that you would go on, stay strong and remain focused on the goal no matter

My Purpose, My Passion, My Drive.

what. We are too much in a hurry to see immediate results for the things we embark on but it shouldn't be. It took God 6 days to create the earth, He didn't do it in a day even if He could, that's because even God understands this singular, universal rule that everything requires a process. It takes a baby 18 years before she is officially termed an adult.
 There's a process.

My husband has taught me a lot of things and determination ranks high on the list. He runs a thriving IT firm today, but it wasn't always rosy, it didn't start out that way but one thing was constant though, He remained true to his vision. I've known several people who had had to close their businesses with fewer challenges than he had at the early stages of the firm. He stuck his guns, despite the odds.
Much earlier in the business he would take about two PCs in his car and offer personalized computer training to people sometimes for free and yet people wouldn't be interested. I must confess that it was very discouraging even for me watching on the sidelines and many times I would suggest to him

"Baby, don't you think it would be better if you just got a job and quit this" and he would respond almost immediately in the negative and emphasize that no way would he go back to paid employment and insist that he would keep doing this for as long as it takes.

I guess you can't argue with a determined spirit and a made up mind.

During the civil rights movement in America in the sixties, a group of demonstrators led by foremost civil rights activists Dr. Martin Luther king marched to the steps of the capital in Montgomery Alabama to demand for voting rights for minorities and nothing was going to deter them. The protesters stood their grounds against white supremacists and hate preachers and pressed on.

Even in the face of danger these protesters were determined to get their message across and to ring it loudly and clearly to the relevant authorities. At the end of the march, the then president of the United State of America, John f Kennedy and other civil rights leaders signed the "Voting Rights ACT of 1965" recalling "the outrage of Selma". That's determination!

Perseverance is another great element in success. It was Henry long fellow that said "if you knock long enough and hard enough at the gate, you are sure to wake up

My Purpose, My Passion, My Drive.

somebody"

In the book of Luke we read the story of a judge whom a widow wearied to the extent that the only solution to his peace of mind was to attend to her petition. Persistence! Knock until the door is opened!

In 1883, John Roebling and his son had an inspiring idea to build a bridge that would connect New York with Long Island. No one believed in the idea, it couldn't possibly be attained, but he wasn't deterred. He and his son persisted and were determined to build. Unfortunately they were involved in a ghastly accident that took his life and left his son brain dead. You'd think it would be the end of the project. How wrong!

Miraculously, the dream didn't die and for 13 long years, with the use of his finger, his son, Washington was able to communicate his intentions to the team of engineers and the bridge was completed. The power of persistence, what seemed impossible could be realized despite the odds.

Your drive is the bedrock of success or failure in your assignment. The first and most important thing to do is to stand up and pursue purpose. Like a man woos a girl till she's his, that's how we must pursue after purpose.

My Purpose, My Passion, My Drive.

The gifts that you posses can only be utilized if you grab opportunities that would be thrown your way because whether you believe it or not , no one on earth is going to have success thrown at them. It's often said that opportunities come but once, but that's not quite true, I'd hate to think that throughout your span of life only one opportunity comes. Opportunities come but certainly not once, how swift you are at seizing the various opportunities would determine how quickly your climb to purpose would be. We must be ready, prepared and aware of the opportunities that are available to us, and take the first steps which are usually little steps to purpose.

Franklin Roosevelt said "to reach a port, we must sail" If you sit and do nothing, your ship would not sail, women must understand that that decision is theirs alone to make. You must seek the necessary knowledge and required training to be the best and harness your talents.

If at the end of the day you cannot justify your existence, you have either failed to recognize your gifts or you have recognized them and have failed to apply them in pursuit of purpose. You must recognize the gift, harness it, expound it and invest the necessary time in developing it.

I have a teenage nephew who plays high school amateur cricket. He invest approximately 4hours everyday and 28 hours every week to cricket; so when he told me , he hopes to go professional with it and be the best cricket player in the country, I believed him. Anything you value, you give it your time. You must invest your time, effort, energy to those talents to ensure success in anything.

Even a farmer would tell you that planting a seed in the ground is only half the job. But the harnessing, tendering and the quality of the soil is what determines if your seed would germinate or not. In our next chapter we would focus on the many reasons why despite our efforts in harnessing our dreams, talents and gifts it just won't grow.

We would use the correlation of soil fertility and seed viability interlink. Metaphorically, the soil would be representing the conditions of our minds, character, hearts, space as it relates to our purpose. We would see how even the noblest of dreams, purposes and gifting can be hindered by our own making because of the condition of our hearts and the readiness to birth purpose.

WORKBOOK
CHAPTER THREE.

This chapter is perhaps the most important chapter in the book as it covers the essence of the book. That is to help as many women as possible to discover why they were created in the first place and answer the question everybody asks- "What on earth am I here for?

Do you believe you were created for a purpose? Explain.

____

____

____

____

____

____

____

Has the book helped you in identifying the reasons why everything is made for a purpose? Give instances

____

____

____

Can you explain the five authorities that have been given to every human being on earth?

Your passion.
How will you describe your current state of fulfillment?

Tick as appropriate.
✍Great, I am currently doing what I enjoy doing.
✍Great I am currently doing what I was born to do.
✍Not so great, it could be better.
✍Not good, I feel I am not utilizing my potential.
✍Frustrated, don't seem to know what to do
✍Not listed above, please list it.

Those at cross roads and still not sure about what they are doing or what they were created to do, don't panic, you are not alone and neither is your quest unique.
Below is an extensive questioner, its goal is to help you identify your passions which is a pointer to purpose. I have

administered it to numerous clients seeking to find life purpose and I hope it would help you as much as it helped them.

FINDING PURPOSE
1.   What do you enjoy doing
        (List top 3 in order of preference)

____

____

____

____

2.   What one thing would you do for free?

____

____

3.   What do you love to talk about?
(List top three in order of preference)

____

____

____

____

4.   What are your values?

____

____

____

____

____

____

5.   What can you not ignore?

____

____

____

6.   What can you invest your last money on?

____

____

____

____

7.   What inspires you and why?

____

____

____

____

____

8.   What problems do you constantly find people asking you to solve

____

____

____

____

____

____

9.   What would you teach for free?

____

____

10.   What would you give willingly for free?

____

____

11.   What matters to you most?

____

____

12.   What causes could you live for?

____

____

____

____

13.   What causes could you die for?

____

____

____

____

14.   If your life were to end today what would be your

       biggest regret?

____

____

____

15.   What would be your biggest joy?

____

____

____

____

16.   Who are you usually drawn to?

____

____

____

____

17.   Describe yourself in one word?

____

____

18.   What character do you struggle the most with?

____

19.   What character do you struggle the least with

____

20.   How do your friends describe you?

____

____

____

____

21.   How does your family describe you?

____

____

____

22.   How do your children describe you?

____

____

____

23.   How do your colleagues describe you?

____

____

---

24.   How does your boss describe you?

25.   How do your subordinates describe you?

26.   Would you describe yourself as an initiator,
        follower or loner?

27.   Do you see you self as an introvert or extrovert?

____

____

28.   What informed your decision above?

____

____

From passion to purpose.
Below are the major determinants of your movement from

passion to purpose.

Determination

1_______2_________3____________4________5
Perseverance

1_______2_________3____________4________5
Diligence

1_______2_________3____________4________5
Enthusiasm

1_______2_________3____________4________5
Integrity of purpose

1_______2_________3____________4________5
Knowledge

1_______2_________3____________4________5

How long you remain in that indeterminate state from

passion to purpose is entirely up to you. Beside these determinants are numbers from 1 to 5, each representing variance from none which is 1 to very high which is 5. Under each determinate circle the number which best represents your current predisposition to the determinant, after which you would add up your total to arrive at your readiness/speed quotient.

1-   None
2-   Minimal
3-   Average
4-   Considerable
5-   Very high.

Interpretation of scores.

6-10   (Not ready and lengthy timespan), a lot of work still needs to be done.

10-15-   (Potentially ready and somewhat lengthy timespan)

15- 20   (Ready and average timespan)
20-26   (Ready and short timespan)
27-30   (Very ready and set for purpose)
Where ever you are on the spectrum, hope is not lost, you can start now from where you are and build on it.
You can get further help and assistance from

www.winnielifeline.com.ng/gethelp

Chapter 4

"I know I'm ready for purpose
When my heart is in
the right place"

Winifred Ayanda

WHY WONT I BIRTH?
(SOIL TRUTHS)

*The Condition Of The Soil Determines
The Potential For Growth.*

My knowledge of agriculture is very limited and somewhat elementary. In fact I must confess that my claim to its knowledge could be ascribed to some stint of compulsory agriculture science at junior high school. I must also confess that it was a very interesting subject for me at the time. Every one of us is either directly or indirectly linked to agriculture. For everything to exist it must feed and feeding is a byproduct of agriculture. Farmers are the life line of the earth. No one can last for long without food. And every farmer knows that it all begins with a seed ie a seed in the soil.

Eighty percent of the success of the growth of any seed is determined by the condition and the quality of the soil. That's why farmers the world over spend billions of dollars ensuring that soil fertility or soil upgradedness is priority. The soil just has to be right for seeds to grow and flourish.

On the flip side, every gift we possess is like a seed and we are the determinants of the extent to which that seed (gift) can fully bloom by the condition of the soil (mindset, heart, character) where the seed resides. How can we seek for a curative measure without a diagnosis ? Let's learn something from the oldest farmer I know.

"… behold a sower went forth to sow, and when he sowed, some seeds fell by the WAYSIDE, and fowls came and devoured them up: others fell upon STONY PLACES, where they had not much earth and forthwith they sprung up,…and when the sun was up, they were scorched and because they had no root, they withered, and some fell among THORNS, and the thorns sprung up and choked them, but others fell into GOOD GROUND and brought forth fruit some hundred, some sixtyfold some thirty fold." Emphasis mine. Mathew13:3-8

Looking at the four kinds of soils mentioned in the parable of the sower in the book of Luke above, we can each identify with at least one of the four different kinds of soils mentioned because they each reflect character and readiness for the birthing of purpose. Let's analyze them individually.

<u>WAYSIDE SOIL</u>.

Here, the bible speaks of seeds falling by the wayside and birds coming to pick them up. Wayside soil is usually hardened by constant traffic of people, animals, vehicles etc. the regular trampling on the soil makes such soil unresponsive and the seeds left exposed at the top of the soil. Such exposure usually is inimical to the seeds because it exposes the seed to opportunist and natural elements.

For Miss Wayside, her unresponsive and seemingly simple ways prevents her from absorbing truth and analyzing situations objectively and dispassionately. She has a false notion that she must be doing something right as people are almost usually drawn to her. In her naivety she misinterprets the attention she gets as a sign of acceptance and hardly sees the need for change or improvement.

Because of Miss Wayside's naturally people pleasing nature she almost always live for others. Her numerous opportunist friends are her greatest undoing. Her life endeavors and achievements are usually someone else's scripts and because of her intense desire and craving for acceptance from every one, she hardly fulfils purpose and rarely reaches peak performance. At some point however, wayside discovers that she has lived her life as cheer leader and has failed to cheer the most important person in her life- herself. The sooner she understands that everyone can't like you and neither can you please everyone; the better for her. Even the Messiah during his earthly pilgrimage couldn't please everyone.

Why won't I birth?

Everyone cannot be your friend and everyone cannot accept you, your message or your purpose. Everyone has a right to their opinions.

Miss Wayside must pray for the spirit of focus and self believe. She must understand that her desires matters as much as others and only when she can have reached a level of self awareness and self worth, only then can she give of herself honestly and truthfully. Any other form of self giving is an abuse of self. Miss Wayside would burnout fast since she only gives and never self nourishes, even the bible preaches giving on the premise that a return is guaranteed. Life must be give and take for it to truly beautiful.

She must remain true to her call and to stay focused. She must learn to mind her own business the way she minds others. Martha in the bible is a typical example of a wayside

woman, who was so focused on serving tables and attending to petty and irrelevant things and even rebuked her sister, Mary, for not waiting tables and assisting her at serving their guest of which Jesus was one. Jesus would later admonished Martha that her sister Mary had chosen a more excellent way by preferring to

Why won't I birth?

nourish herself by learning at his feet rather than waiting on tables. Surprised! Well don't be.

We read much later however how she was among the women at the forefront of the apostolic revival. She must have learnt something ie to give of yourself first and then of your fullness and completeness give to others.

STONY OR ROCKY SOIL

These are usually soil just resting on the surface of the rock and are not very deep. The thin layer of dust or soil allows the seeds to germinate quickly but that growth will be short lived because of the shallow soil.

At first glance, Miss Rocky may seem God sent, but her seemingly quick assistance and unsolicited volunteering soon comes to an abrupt end much to your chagrin. These women are usually lacking in the determination department. Their commitment is usually superficial. They volunteer quickly and back off almost immediately. Miss rocky is usually the first one to volunteer for anything in a group and would almost always be the first one to quit. She hardly analyzes the whole situation because she is usually in a
haste to get things done quickly.

Why won't I birth?

Purpose cannot bear in such woman because she neither has the tenacity nor the rugged determination to follow through on her primary assignment. Her apparent zeal is deceptive, her assistance shallow and her help eventually becomes a burden. Fancy selecting a team made up of over 50% Miss rocky, consider your project team as good as 50% short because they would most definitely pull out. They come across promising at first and steadily decline to off mode.

If you are looking for the people who come up with the most ideas, suggestions and project concepts; it's Miss Rocky! She would embark on 1001 projects and complete zero.

But Miss Rocky can find a way out of frivolity if only she can allow the Holy Spirit to direct and lead her through the one and the most important assignment in her life which in her purpose.

Saphira in the bible is a typical example of Miss Rocky, she was neither cajoled nor coerced into providing for the early church but she fell short of the required or acceptable standard for provision at the time in the early church by falsely declaring her donations as total whereas she had withheld part.

<u>*Why won't I birth?*</u>

One may be quick to wonder why she would do that considering the fact that she wasn't under any obligation to donate more than she felt she could give. It's been believed
that she in collusion with her husband may have quickly gone ahead to make big promises that they were later reluctant to fulfill which is very typical of all stony and rocky types.

That singular act of deception didn't go down well with the apostle Peter and it caused Saphira to go to her early grave! Now you don't necessary have to have such a tragic ending. Miss rocky's way out is to let the Holy Spirit guide her in taking and making right decisions and sticking through with it.

AMONG THORNS

Some seed fell among thorns. Here, the seeds actually fell among relatively good soil but because of the presence of thorns they choked up the seeds. They struggled with the seeds to claim the limited nutrients that are necessary for growth and eventually swallowed up the seed. Of all the three soils mentioned, Miss Thorny has the most potential however her anxiety and care for irrelevant things other than things that gear her towards purpose is her greatest undoing.

Why won't I birth?

Nobody has more excuses than Miss Thorny. She has a million and one reasons why she can't do one thing or the other. She`s on a mission to defend her excuses; she refuses to take responsibilities for her actions or inactions because in her mind;   she didn't have a fair deal in life; her parents were poor; her education wasn't right, her growing up was tough, etc!
She`s always short for time for almost everything and she`s got ready made answers and excuses for everything. It's not unusual to hear reasons like: "Oh; I would have done it but my son is very demanding".

Or "Sorry; have to take charlotte to ballet class, maybe next time".

Or yet again, "I`ll finish college once I've got a bit more free time;

Excuses; excuses; excuses! ; Excuses be gone!. Miss Thorny is choked on her own excuses and she seldom sees anything wrong with that, at least, she gave a reason!

Working with Miss Thorny is always a chore. The sooner Miss Thorny gets that she`s not the only one on the planet with a reason why things might have been

<u>Why won't I birth?</u>

postponed, or why project shouldn`t be embarked upon, the better for her.

Miss Thorny would never actually reach potential because for her; there is a reason why the time is never right.

But there`s still hope for Miss Thorny; others have towed her path and have decided to say **NO** to excuses and to take up the challenge that pursuing purpose demands no matter what.

It's not uncommon for lots of women to find themselves as
Miss Thorny because of the huge responsibilities and roles women have to joggle in society but we must remember we owe it to the very people we love and are trying to be there for to live our lives to the fullest by living in purpose.

GOOD SOIL

I know I'm ready to birth purpose when my heart is in the right place. Miss Good soil is a woman ready to birth purpose, not because all conditions are perfect but because she has perfected all conditions.

Interestingly, the parable when speaking on the returns

Why won't I birth?

on the growth of the seeds on this soil it didn't say they all yielded 100% but rather that they yielded differently, some 30%, some 60% while others yielded 100%.

This simply means that the extent to which you fulfill your purpose is directly proportionate to the extent of your exaction and investment in its fulfillment. 100% exaction and investment yields 100% and so on.

Miss Good soil has learnt how to master her emotions; she understands who she is, whose she is and who she is called to be. She understands that whatever her weaknesses, she has it made up in her strengths. She knows how to choose her battles and she knows who her friends are. She has learnt her life's lessons and is ready to give of herself to humanity.

Miss Good soil is not your typical woman, she most certainly isn't politically correct, and she understands that to live her life to the fullest and live purpose she must set herself on a course that is almost always against the typical expectations of societal norms. In her mind she can and must be all that she is destined to be. She is comfortable in her skin and knows that she is perfectly made for her assignment. On her assignment, she takes no prisoners and goes about the pursuit regardless of whose ox is goad. She is a phenomenal

Why won't I birth?

woman who understands that she is MADE **DIFFERENT** but no less inferior or superior to her male counterpart. She is confident in the originality of her essence and in the distinctiveness of her call and more importantly her specific role in the overall scheme of things

One thing going for Miss Goodsoil is that she would not only fulfill purpose but would also inspire others to fulfill theirs. By virtue of reading this book, I know you aspire to be Miss Good soil, that is of course if you aren't one already. The reason being that she is constantly searching ways of enriching herself and quickening her attainment of purpose through her quest for knowledge and truth.

Know that no one is born ready to birth purpose despite that they possess all necessary tools to birth purpose. It takes preparation, determination, focus, perseverance and the readiness of your mind to birth purpose. Start now to unlock purpose from within. The signs are all around you.

Through your journey to purpose we encounter different types of people. In our next chapter we shall be examining the various people that can make or mar our

WORKBOOK
CHAPTER FOUR.

This chapter is all about the heart (the soil) and birthing purpose. Until you deal with your heart, character, purpose may be far from you. From the classic story of the parable of the sower in the book of Matthew, this chapter draws its inspiration from. As you work on this workbook, it is important that you discover your soil type, work on it, and cultivate it until it is ready to birth purpose,
From the chapter you just read, what soil type do you think you are and why?

____

____

____

____

____

____

____

____

____

____

Why won't I birth?

Can you list some of the ways that you have displayed some of the traits similar to this soil type?

____

____

____

____

Can you list some of the ways the book has been able to help you find some solutions to the flaws of this soil type?

____

____

____

____

____

____

____

____

____

____

____

What steps would you take starting from now to ensure
that you become Miss Good soil and ready to birth
purpose?

Chapter

5

> "I truly believe… everyone that
> We meet is put in our path for a
> Purpose. There are no
> Accidents".
>
> *Marta gibbs.*

LIFTERS AND DRIFTERS.

"There would always be the lifters,
those pulling you towards purpose and the drifters ,
those pulling you away from purpose."

As we journey through life we encounter people, the lifters (those who pull us closer to purpose) and the drifters (those who pull us away from purpose)

Everyone we meet would fall into those two categories, no matter who they are; they maybe family; friends; acquaintances; colleagues; neighbours and even the "haters". It would be naïve to think that the people in your life don't really matter or determine your fulfillment of purpose.

In Exodus; God was giving Moses his life`s purpose and Moses felt extremely inadequate especially because of his speech impairment. His fears were legitimate, if he was to be a spokesman for a nation, he should at least be articulate. He was quick to point out this short coming to God, but do you think God didn't already know that? In response to his plea for a rethink for his assignment, God directed his attention to his brother Aaron and told him that his brother would help him out with that. God needed the heart of Moses but the voice of Aaron his brother. Aaron was a lifter alright, he was fundamental to Moses' successful attainment of purpose.

In the story of David; in his pursuit for purpose, ironically , an unlikely friend, his rival's son Jonathan;

became his number one championeer for his fulfillment of purpose. He kept David one step ahead of his number one enemy in his fulfillment of purpose!

President Barrack Obama of the USA says he owes his success to his single mother. Simon Cowell; Richard Branson; David Beckham; they all lay their claim to success to their mothers.
Hear what Richard Branson had to say about his mother`s influence in his life.

"...I learned a lot about this from my mother; who is a very energetic and strong-willed individual. I`m thankful for the life lesson she taught me; without which I would probably not be where I am today. I always wanted to go out there and prove myself; but I was very shy when I was young and it was clear that I would have to master this if I was going to succeed. My timidity could have easily held me back if she hadn't helped me come out of my shell. She feels that shyness is very selfish; as it means you are only thinking of yourself, she was very insistent that I look adults in the eye and shake their hands; and carry on conversations with guests at <u>dinners an</u>d at parties; no excuses."

On the flip side; sometimes people may also go the opposite direction of purpose through their

<u>*Lifters and drifters*</u>

acquaintance; colleagues; friends; family. Each of these people; the lifters and drifters come into your life some for a season others for a reason and some others are with you for a lifetime.

LIFTERS

Lifters gear you closer to purpose and some may be intentionally while others may be unintentionally. Some lifters are in your life for a lifetime; others come in a season or period in your life and some you just meet casually, and make the most profound impression in your life. They are basically four types of lifters you meet in your lifetime. They are: seasonal, social, lifetime and unintentional lifters.

SEASONAL LIFTERS.

These lifters come to your life at a particular time or season in your life. Everybody's life got seasons and in all of these seasons, lifters come along.

In the story of the widow of Zarepth, the young widow encountered a prophet by the name of Elijah; she was at her wit end and in her season of anguish she cried out to the servant of God for an immediate intervention to her plight, failure of which would result in death of not only her but her entire household.

The prophet was able to miraculously intervene which resulted in her thriving and bumming oil business that saw her not only surviving but thriving exceptionally well. Talk about a God-sent lifter at her season of distress. His singular intervention was able to transform her from a needy widow to a business magnate in an instant!

Another seasonal lifter is Ananias of Paul. Paul had been blinded by an encounter with the Lord, and in this season of
deep reflection and conviction, Ananias was sent to restore his sight and empower him with the Holy Spirit to be able to fulfill his purpose. Paul went on to be an apostle of faith and the author of two thirds of the New Testament.

SOCIAL LIFTERS (REASON)

Theses lifters are peculiar and by far the most self-seeking of all lifters but self-seeking in a good way. In their quest to promote their agendas, belief and causes, they assemble in groups, social events, caucuses all with intent to gain, but in the end they all gain. They all share common and unifying interest and they each look out for the growth of that belief or cause which ultimately results to individual growth as well as collective growth. They belief strongly in the notion that together they can achieve more. Running together as a team is a whole lot quicker than if you were to journey alone.

Several associations exist all over the world all of which are specifically geared towards specific causes, the civil rights movement, justice movements, civil liberty organizations, women and child rights organizations, religious organizations, professional and political associations are all platforms to gear people towards attainment of purpose when individuals either engage in the participation of these social engagements which further their causes and invariably leads them towards purpose.

UNINTENTIONAL LIFTERS.

Call them anything you like, these ones are the least likely recognized of the lifters because they initially don't set out to lift. As a matter of fact they actually set out with the intention to destroy and demoralize but to some of their targets the opposite is actually achieved, no porn intended. Some people call them "haters". They are the unlikely ones who propel you to want to disappoint their expectations, their continuous hounding, putting down and setting of boobie traps along your journey to purpose, unknowingly make you better, stronger, and more prepared to face life's challenges and ultimately cause you to fulfill purpose.

I met a lady once who said she has her elementary school teacher to thank for the way she turned out. She confided in me that she was on a secret mission to prove her teacher wrong that good things can come from the least expected places. Many of you may be just like her with your own unique story.

Some other unintentional lifters are a bit more forceful than that, in the book of Nehemiah, we read about Nehemiah's passion to build the walls of Jerusalem and how he got all the necessary help even from the king, however he had two very persistent haters named Samballat and Tobhias who were hell bent on ensuring that Nehemiah wouldn't achieve his dream.

They employed every resource within their power: money, influence, sarcasm, blackmail, and even death threat but guess what? The more they lashed on, the more the work progressed the more Nehemiah and his team advanced in building more united than ever until the wall was built and even early than anticipated. Haters would always be there that's not the new thing but your reaction to their schemes is what would determine if you use them as a stepping stone to purpose and not a stumbling block to purpose.

LIFETIME LIFTERS.

These aren't going anywhere soon, as a matter of fact they aren't going anywhere period!

You're stuck with them but in a good way; they are the ones that are cheering you on no matter what; I can hear you say your mum; Believe it or not; lifetime lifters are the reason you make it against all odds.

Some are family; others are friends who have become more like family, they only see the good and potential in you. They are usually the ones you fall back on during the low times.

There was a season in my life where nothing mattered to me anymore and I had almost given up on everything, it took one of my lifelong lifters to bring me back on track. Her letter remains with me till today.

Lifters and drifters

Let me share it with you.

> *My dear sister,*
> *I know how you must feel right*
> *now but I want you to know that*
> *there is a treasure within you that*
> *must not be wasted. You must never*
> *lose focus. A lot of destinies are tied*
> *to you. You must not disappoint*
> *destiny. Love you to shreads,*
> *Akhi.*

Know that God is your number one life time lifter. He says he would be with you through thick and thin and He would never leave you nor forsake you. He means exactly what he says.

DRIFTERS.

The other set of people you meet on your journey to purpose are the drifters. They are generally only two kinds of drifters and they are the intentional and unintentional drifters.

UNINTENTIONAL DRIFTERS

Like unintentional lifters, the unintentional drifters don't present themselves with the intension to drift. They are friends that hang around you and may mean well but their lifestyles, dispositions and attitudes are at crossroads with your purpose and because you may not be at liberty to hack them out of your life and prevent them from having access to your world, they are ever present. You have a responsibility to ensure that these drifters know that you have an assignment to pursue and your time is much too valuable to waste. This must be followed through persistently until such drifters get the message loud and clear.

It would be tough at first but later on they would eventually get it. Now, how they respond to your stance should not be a cause of worry to you because you know where exactly you are going.

Jesus was going about his business when some group of people approached him and said "teacher, your family is here," and jesus said " who is my mother" Jesus' response to that showed us how our reaction should be to any distraction on our journey to purpose irrespective of who it may be. Now, don't get me wrong here, no one is advocating shunning family, we have seen in the earlier chapters how vital family is in our molding for purpose, but family must never be a reason for derailing of purpose.

You have to politely tell friends and family that you are going about your assignment both in words and actions and no distractions are permitted.

I get asked time again how do I let parasitic friends off my back so I could move on with what I've got to do? And I tell them that people would constantly test your resolve to saying enough and no more. Even children do this all the time with the adults in their lives. You must be serious about letting them know that you mean business first by telling and secondly by showing, and eventually the message is passed across.

INTENTIONAL DRIFTERS.
These are on a mission to ensure that you don't fulfill your purpose. The peculiar thing about these ones is that their success is in direct proportion to your reactions.

There is a thin line between an unintentional lifter and an intentional drifter which as I said earlier is directionally proportional to your reaction. Your reactions to these types of drifters would ultimately determine how well their mission is executed.

You have the power to determine the extent an intentional drifter plays in your life by being decisive and resolute in your resolve to fulfilling purpose no matter what. Everyone is faced with both drifters and lifters in their pursuit of purpose. But remember no one can stop purpose except by the powers you have extended to them. And even though some may have a claim to success to one lifter or the other, the ultimate responsibility rest on your table. You are the one who has to want it bad enough. So what's stopping you?

In our last chapter we would look at some phenomenal women who triumphed against all odds and read through how ordinary women did extraordinary things and accomplished feats and changed their world. I hope their stories would inspire you the way they inspired me.

WORKBOOK
CHAPTER FIVE.

This chapter is all about the lifters (those that pull you towards purpose) and the drifters those that pull you away from purpose.
Haven read through this chapter, can you identify those in your life that are lifters?

Lifters and drifters

Can you identify the drifters in your life?

<u>*Lifters and drifters*</u>

Can you list some of the conscious steps you are going to take to ensure that you encourage the lifters in your life .

____

____

____

____

____

____

____

____

____

____

Can you list some of the conscious steps you are going
to take to ensure that you let go of the drifters in your
life.

____

____

____

____

____

____

____

____

____

____

____

____

____

____

Chapter
6
AGAINST ALL ODDS

culled from www.biographyonline.net

"Because they did it; we too can".

We can identify with almost all of these women because they reflect the genuity of our every day struggle, handling our inner demands, they transcended every known barrier, every limitation and all manners of discrimination to break free from societal expectations and took their destinies in their own hands.

If after they all have made it in insurmountable circumstances and you still don't make it, know woman that you failed not because of limitations but because you gave u on your purpose before it could bear. Next time you are tempted to give up on purpose, think again on the selfishness of that decision and the ripple effect it would have on your generation and generations yet unborn because , you had a a chance at the reins of destiny and chose to despise it.,

Keep in mind that they just like most of us were born disadvantaged but applied the basic principle of determination; passion, love of God and humanity coupled with a strong pursuit of purpose. ANYONE CAN WIN, IF YOU WANT TO. Nobody said winning was easy but it's worth it.

These women fought for what they believed and won and we are better for it. Nothing good comes easy, life is

Against all odds

thrust with loads of disappointments as well as opportunities. You too can follow their lead and fill up the gap for others to learn from you.

Wake up every morning with the awareness that purpose cant wait and you have to fulfill it no matter what. Say to yourself, if I were to dro dead today, who would have benefitted from my existence?, whose life would I have impacted, what cause would suffer from my loss or im I just another space occupier.

So woman; go ahead; run; a life is counting on you. You are the one we`ve been waiting for.

WOMEN OF PURPOSE & PASSION

FOLORUNSHO ALAKIJA is a Nigerian businesswoman who is the richest woman of African descent in the world. Her tremendous wealth is touching lives of venerable children and women particularly in Africa.

Her inspirational story has inspired a whole lot of African girls that they can aspire to any height they put their mind to.

ROSA PARKS is usually referred to as the first lady of civil rights; she was a pioneer of civil right in a racially segregated Alabama in 1950`s. in 1955; she refused to give away her seat to a white passer in a bus in Montgomery; Alabama thereby; disobeying the bus driver`s orders. This act of hers sparked the Montgomery bus Boycott.

HELEN KELLER at a very young age, Helen became deaf and blind. Overcoming the frustration of losing both sight
and hearing she has inspired a lot of girls and people generally in achieving anything they desire despite seemingly enormous physical and social challenges.

HAMIT TUBMAN is a Christian who escaped slavery and went on to lead an influential movement within the Underground Railroad.

MIRIAM MAKEBA FONDLY REFERRED TO AS MAMA AFRICA was a prominently outspoken and visible opponent of South Africa's apartheid regime. Miriam Makeba was not only involved in radical activity against apartheid but also in the civil rights movement and then black power.

WANGARI MAATHAI is a Kenyan born environmentalist, who is also a prodemocracy activist and women`s right campaigner. She was awarded a

Nobel peace prize for efforts to prevent conflict through protection of scare resources.

ROSALIND RUIKER`S can be refered to as the mother of modern prayer. Through her works ,conversing with God changed the way we pray; and showed Christians how to talk to God as a friend; conversationally.

HELENA RUBINSTEIN immigrated to Australia in 1902 without any money or the ability to speak in English. Thereafter she founded one of the world`s first cosmetic companies.. Following that she became the world`s richest at
the time which she used to support charitable enterprises in the field of education, arts and health.

MARGARET THATCHER is usually referred to as the iron lady for her leadership style and uncompromising policies. She was loved and hated equally for some of her controversial policies but she never gave up,. From her humbly background to graduating from oxford to becoming a barrister; she went on to becoming Britain first and to date; only female prime minister elected in 1979 and the 5th longest serving leader

QUEEN NZINGA POPULARLY KNOWN AS THE REFORMIST FROM ANGOLA WHO ORGANIZED a powerful guerrilla army, conquered some of her enemies and developed alliances to control the slave routes. She even allied with the Dutch to help her stop the Portuguese advancement. After a series of decisive setbacks, Nzinga had to negotiate a peace treaty with the Portuguese, but still refused to pay tribute to the Portuguese king.

FLORENCE NIGHTINGALE REFERRED TO AS "The lady with the lamp". She nursed wounded soldiers during the Crimean war. Her dedication to the profession changed public's perception about the nursing profession.

AMELIA EARHART WAS THE FIRST WOMAN to fly solo across the Atlantic in 1932 from Hawaii to California. She embarked upon her lifelong dream of flying across the world in 1937; however; her flight went missing and she was never seen again.

MARY WOLLSTONECRAFT IS AN English author, her tract "A Vindication of the Rights of Women" laid down a clear moral and practical basis for extending human and political rights to women. – A true pioneer in the struggle for female suffrage.

MARIE CURIE famously known as "Madame Curie"is a polish – French physicist and chemist; she was the first person to have received two Nobel prizes and the first female professor at the university of Paris.she helped to develop the first xray machines.

MARY MAGDALENE was one of Jesus most devoted followers she showed us how to worship the lord. Mary Magdalene stood near Jesus at his crucifixion and was the first to witness his resurrection.

JANE AUSTEN is one of the most popular female authors. Jane Austen wrote several novels, which remain highly popular today. These include "Pride and Prejudice" "Emma" and "Northanger Abbey". Jane Austen wrote at a time when female writers were not so high profile, helping pave the way for future female writers.

HARRIET BEECHER STOWE   A lifelong anti slavery campaigner. Her novel "Uncle Tom's Cabin" was a best seller and helped to popularise the anti slavery campaign. Abraham Lincoln would later remark her books were a major factor behind the American civil war.

ELIZABETH BLACKWELL was the first women to receive a medical degree in America and the first women to be on the UK medical register. Blackwell helped to break down social barriers, enabling women to be accepted as doctors.

EMILY MURPHY was the first women magistrate in the British Empire. In 1927 she joined forces with four other Canadian women who sought to challenge an old Canadian law that said, "women should not be counted as persons"

COCO CHANEL is a French fashion designer. One of the most innovative fashion designers, Coco Chanel was instrumental in defining feminine style and dress during the 20th Century. Her ideas were revolutionary; in particular she often took traditionally male clothes and redesigned them for the benefit of women.

ELEANOR ROOSEVELT Wife and political aide of American president F.D.Roosevelt. In her own right Eleanor made a significant contribution to the field of human rights, a topic she campaigned upon throughout her life. As head of UN human rights commission she helped to draft the 1948
UN declaration of human rights.

Against all odds

MOTHER TERESA is an Albanian nun who devoted her entire   life to the service of the poor and dispossessed. She is known globally for her selfless service to others. Through her Missionary of Charities organisation she personally cared for thousands of sick and dying people in Calcutta. She was awarded the Nobel Peace prize in 1979.

DOROTHY HODGKIN is a British chemist. Hodgkin was awarded the Nobel prize for her work on critical discoveries of the structure of both penicillin and later insulin.   These   discoveries   led   to   significant improvements in health care. An outstanding chemist, Dorothy also devoted a large section of her life to the peace movement and promoting nuclear disarmament. **Eva Peron** – Eva Peron was widely loved by the ordinary people of Argentina. She campaigned tirelessly for both the poor and for the extension of women's rights. She died aged only 32 in 1952.

BETTY FRIEDAN – American social activist and leading feminist figure of the 1960s; she wrote the best-selling book "The Feminine Mystique" Friedan campaigned for an extension of female rights and an end to sexual discrimination.

ANNE FRANK – Dutch / Jewish author. Anne Frank's diary is one of the most widely read books in the world. It
reveals the thoughts of a young, yet surprisingly mature 13-year-old girl, confined to a secret hiding place. "Despite everything, I believe that people are really good at heart."

BETTY WILLIAMS Together with Mairead Corrigan, Betty Williams campaigned to bring an end to the sectarian violence of Northern Ireland. They founded the Community for Peace and were awarded the Nobel Peace Prize in 1977 (post dated for 1976)
Billie Jean King American tennis player. Billie Jean King was one of the greatest female tennis champions, who also battled for equal pay for women. She won 67 professional titles including 20 titles at Wimbledon.

SHIRIN EBADI An Iranian lawyer, Ebadi has fought for human rights in Iran – representing political dissidents and founding initiatives to promote democracy and human rights. Awarded the Nobel Peace Prize in 2003.

BENAZIR BHUTTO The first female prime minister of a Muslim country. She helped to move Pakistan from a dictatorship to democracy becoming Prime Minister in 1988. She sought to implement social reforms, in particular helping women and the poor. She was assassinated in 2007.

OPRAH WINFREY – American chat show host. Oprah Winfrey was the first woman to own her own talk show. Her show and book club are very influential, focusing on issues
facing American women. she continues to inspire women the world over.

DIANA, PRINCESS OF WALES   British Royal princess who was noted for her humanitarian charity work. Despite her troubled marriage to Prince Charles, she was popular for her natural sympathy with the poor and marginalised from society.

TEGLA LOROUPE Kenyan athlete. Loroupe held the women's marathon world record and won many prestigious marathons. Since retiring from running, she has devoted herself to various initiatives promoting peace, education and women's rights. In her native Kenya, her Peace Race and Peace Foundation have been widely praised for helping to end tribal conflict.

MALALA YOUSAFZAI is a Pakistani schoolgirl who defied threats of the Taliban to campaign for the right to education. She survived being shot in the head by the Taliban and has become a global advocate for women's rights, especially the right to education.

HILARY CLINTON US Secretary of State 2009-2013. First lady during Bill Clinton's presidency and democratic candidate for President in 2008 and 2016.

ANGELA MERKEL Merkel has been chancellor of Germany since 2005 and the de facto leader of the European Union during financial crisis.
AUNG SAN SUU KYI Burmese democrat and civil rights
 activist.

YAA ASANTEWA ALSO KNOWN AS THE COMMANDER IN CHIEF. No woman is known in the history of the African reactions and responses to European power better than Nana Yaa Asantewa of the Asante state Edweso in Ghana. She was the military leader of what is known as the 'Yaa Asantewa War', which was the last war between the Asante and the British, and during which she became referred to by the British as the 'Joan D'Arc of Africa'.

MAYA ANGELOU – Modern American poet and writer and activist. Her writings have impacted a whole generation of people.

SERENA WILLIAMS American tennis player. Williams has won 19 single grand slam titles, making her the most successful female player of her generation.

And of course you, WOMAN OF PURPOSE, go ahead I believe in you.

culled from www.biographyonline.net

WORKBOOK
CHAPTER SIX.

Dear phenomenal woman, I'll end this session by asking you to write a love letter to your new self because you deserve it. Be sure to include some affirmations to your new life!

Dear ____________

____

____

____

____

____

____

____

____

____

____

____

____

If this book has touched your life, send me an email info@winifredayanda.com and share your personal story. For more information and counselling visit www.winifredayanda.com. May God bless and enrich your life as you begin your journey to purpose.

About The Author

Winnie is a Certified Directional Life Coach and Counselor. She is the Resident Pastor, BreakingForth Church, Nigeria and the Lead Coach, WLC Coaching & Counseling Agency. Winnie is also the convener of Women Helping Women (WHW) Initiative and President of the Mogul Women Investment Club. She was awarded Woman Of the Year 2019 by the The Intellects Giants Award (TIGA) Academy for her outstanding contribution to empowerment of women in all strata of the society. An author of several inspirational books, a trainer, teacher of God's word and Speaker.

For bookings and a list of speaking presentations and topics, please email her at info@winifredayanda.com or visit her website www.winifredayanda.com for more information.

Winnie is happily married with children.

Contact Information

Breakingforth Church , Lagos Nigeria.
28, Olatunde Onimole Street, Aguda,
Surulere Lagos, Nigeria.
Telephone: 234-909-2820-968, 234-817-6333-717.